M000159243

the little book of
INSPIRATION

lucy lane

summersdale

THE LITTLE BOOK OF INSPIRATION

Copyright © Summersdale Publishers Ltd, 2016

With research by Katherine Bassford

Summersdale Publishers Ltd
46 West Street
Chichester
West Sussex
PO19 1RP
UK

www.summersdale.com

Printed and bound in the Czech Republic

ISBN: 978-1-84953-843-5

Substantial discounts on bulk quantities of Summersdale books are available to corporations, professional associations and other organisations. For details contact general enquiries: telephone: +44 (0) 1243 771107, fax: +44 (0) 1243 786300 or email: enquiries@summersdale.com.

INTRODUCTION

We all want to feel joy, passion and purpose in our lives, but it can be hard to stay motivated and enthusiastic when faced with the demands of everyday life. Thankfully, there is inspiration all around us, whether you find it while sleeping under the stars, by spending time with optimistic people, or in reviving a long-lost ambition. New experiences can open the floodgates to fresh perspectives and ideas, so if you're feeling stuck or uninspired, dip into this little book and try something new today. These motivating quotes and simple tips are designed to help you tap into your creativity, reignite your passion, and open your eyes to exciting new possibilities.

WRITE A
BUCKET LIST

It's easy to get caught up in a flurry of day-to-day activities and forget what you really want from life. A 'bucket list' is a list of all the goals and dreams you want to achieve in your lifetime, and can be a great way of reminding you of what's really important. To create your list, sit down and think of all the things you want to do, see, feel and experience. Keep going until you have at least 100 items on your list. If you find yourself stuck, you may be mentally limiting yourself. Let yourself go – what would you do if you had unlimited time, money and resources? What have you always wanted to do but not yet done? Items on your list may be 'big', such as travelling around the world or running a marathon, or 'small', such as watching a sunrise or seeing your favourite band play live. Once you've written your list, start ticking off the goals you achieve and add any new ones that come to mind. Writing a bucket list should encourage you to live life to the full and look forward to the days ahead with renewed enthusiasm.

Catch the trade
wind in your sails.
Explore. **Dream**.
Discover.

H. Jackson Brown Jr

BREAK FROM THE ORDINARY

If you're stuck in the same old routine, it might be time to try something new. Spend a day (or at least a few hours) purposely departing from your normal routine: tune in to a different radio station, take an alternate route to work, try a new cafe or restaurant, visit an unusual shop or say 'hi' to a neighbour you don't normally talk to. Take every opportunity to experience your world in brand new ways. By widening your perspective, you'll expose yourself to new ideas and inspirations.

Happiness is a way of travel, not a destination.

Roy M. Goodman

ALL LIFE IS AN EXPERIMENT. THE MORE EXPERIMENTS YOU MAKE, THE BETTER.

Ralph Waldo Emerson

SAY YES

If you're feeling uninspired, doing something spontaneous may not be the most obvious solution. However, doing something fun or unusual may be just what you need to lift your spirits. A good way to practise this is to start saying 'yes' to things. If you're invited to a party that you wouldn't normally attend, say 'yes' and make yourself go. If you walk past a poster advertising a dance or photography class you've always secretly wanted to try, sign up the second you get home. By saying 'yes' to possibilities that are placed before you, you'll open your world to new people, places and experiences. This will probably entail stepping out of your comfort zone but the benefits include more spontaneity, excitement and adventure. Try saying 'yes' to life for an hour, a day or a month and see what happens.

Look on every **exit** as being an **entrance** somewhere else.

Tom Stoppard

The foolish man
seeks happiness in
the distance, the wise
grows it under his feet.

J. Robert Oppenheimer

CREATE A BUZZ

One of the biggest challenges with meeting goals is finding the motivation to keep going. This can feel like an uphill struggle at times, but there are simple tricks that can help you generate energy and excitement to help propel you towards your dream. Whether you dream of entering a triathlon or starting a new business, seek inspiration from others. Talk to your partner about your idea or share your thoughts with a supportive friend. Chat to like-minded people via local clubs or online forums. Imagine what it would feel like to achieve your ambition, and visualise yourself succeeding. Motivation is not a constant thing – it will come and go – but by surrounding yourself with positive people and images, you'll generate the buzz and excitement that will keep you moving towards your goal.

BE THE CALM CENTRE IN THE RAGING FLOW OF LIFE.

Leo Babauta

SAVOUR A SUNRISE

Have you ever taken the time to sit and watch a sunrise? This wonder of nature can fill you with awe and reverence. Check the weather, pick a clear day and find a beautiful spot. The sun rises in the east and sets in the west, so make sure you have a clear view. Arrive in plenty of time, so you can make the most of the experience. Wrap up warm, sit down with a friend or loved one, and enjoy. You won't need to go back to bed afterwards – you'll be inspired and ready to take on the day.

SECRET DESIRES

Is there something you've secretly always wanted to try? Many of us have heartfelt desires we have buried deep inside us. Maybe you've always wanted to learn to dance, play the drums or go rock climbing? Think of something you've always longed to do and find a way to experience it in some way. Booking a lesson or taster session may mean stepping out of your comfort zone for a while, but it will boost your confidence, light up your soul, and fill you with a sense of accomplishment. No matter how things turn out, you'll know you had the courage to try something new. You'll realise the only thing holding you back is your thinking – and with this thought, an exciting new world will start to open up to you.

Your mind is your instrument. Learn to be its master and not its slave.

Remez Sasson

Try to be like the turtle –
at ease in your own shell.

Bill Copeland

EXPRESS YOURSELF

Being creative is a great way to express your thoughts, feelings and ideas. It can help you make sense of your experiences and the world around you. Try expressing yourself creatively in a way you've never done before, such as flower arranging, singing or dancing, for example. There are adult education classes in all sorts of subjects, but if you'd rather not commit to a class, you could get a How To book out from the library, watch an instructional DVD, or take up a creative hobby you can learn by yourself at home, such as cake decorating. Whatever you do, choose something that sounds like fun. Remember, anyone can be creative, and no matter the outcome, if you're embracing this side of your personality you're always winning. Experimenting with new or unusual creative outlets can lead to new thoughts and unexpected breakthroughs. At the very least, you'll have a blast.

THE POWER OF
THE DOODLE

Reconnect with your inner child and start doodling. Experts say doodling is a quick and effective way to switch off your thinking and unleash your creativity. Whatever you draw – whether you create shapes, patterns, or letters – a doodle is not supposed to be a work of art, so you can relax and just have fun expressing yourself. Place a pad of paper and some pens on your desk or beside your bed, so that you can pick up a pen and let your mind wander whenever you feel the urge.

EVERYTHING YOU DO CAN BE DONE BETTER FROM A PLACE OF RELAXATION.

Stephen C. Paul

Energy and persistence conquer all things.

Benjamin Franklin

With the new day
comes new strength
and new thoughts.

Eleanor Roosevelt

A BIRTHDAY EVERY DAY!

Our birthday is often one of the most memorable days of the year, whether we opt for a meal in a restaurant, a party at home, or a day out with family or friends. Birthdays are a chance to celebrate life, to feel special, and to spend quality time with loved ones. So why wait another 364 days to enjoy life to the fullest? Why not celebrate each day with the magic of a birthday? Treat yourself to something nice – book a massage or buy yourself a gift, for example. Or turn the tables and treat someone else: buy a big helium balloon for a friend or bake them a cake for no reason other than to show your appreciation. It needn't cost lots of money: simply making time to be with loved ones or inviting a friend around for a meal can be just as special. Live each day as if it's your birthday and you'll experience a year full of memorable days.

IT DOES NOT
MATTER HOW
SLOWLY YOU GO
AS LONG AS YOU
DO NOT STOP.

Confucius

CAPTURING BEAUTY

Take a camera outside and photograph anything that looks beautiful to you. This could be a stunning view or a piece of architecture, or it could be something more obscure such as a colourful fabric, the texture of rust, or an old door. By actively looking for beautiful things in your environment, you'll train your brain to notice feel-good people, places and objects and you'll start to see more and more of the beauty that surrounds you.

You can't wait for **inspiration**. You have to go after it with a club.

Jack London

Optimism is the faith that leads to **achievement**. Nothing can be done without hope and **confidence**.

Helen Keller

WRITE A LOVE LIST

It's easy to take things for granted in life. A simple way to amplify your feeling of gratitude and abundance is to write a Love List. Sit down with a pen and paper and make a list of everything that you are passionate about. Don't limit yourself. This is about listing all the things YOU love, not what other people think. Include all the things, people, places and concepts that bring you joy and make your heart sing. These items can be as big or as small as you like. Write your list in a special notebook and review it regularly. It's easy to be bogged down by our To Do lists and endless obligations. Writing a Love List will help reconnect you with the myriad things that make your life happier – from being greeted in the morning by your dog to walking outside in the sunshine.

WATCH TED

If you're in need of inspiration, head to www.ted.com. TED is a non-profit organisation devoted to spreading ideas in the form of short, powerful talks by the world's most inspired thinkers. On the TED website you'll discover talks on every conceivable topic, from science to art to global issues. You can browse the library of 2,000+ talks and speakers and engage with a community of like-minded curious souls on their TED Conversations platform.

THE PREREQUISITE
FOR ME IS TO
KEEP MY WELL OF
IDEAS FULL. THIS
MEANS LIVING
AS FULL AND
VARIED A LIFE
AS POSSIBLE.

Michael Morpurgo

As soon as you start
to pursue a **dream**,
your life wakes up
and everything has
meaning.

Barbara Sher

If we all did the things
we are capable of, we
would astound ourselves.

Thomas Edison

CHOOSE A NEW HABIT

On average, it takes around two months before a new behaviour becomes a habit. Make today the day you embrace a new healthy habit that has the power to change your life for the better. You could commit to a weekly yoga class, make a healthy packed lunch to take to work, or meditate for five minutes every night. Whatever you choose, make sure it's something do-able. Setting big goals is exciting but can feel daunting, so taking baby steps can greatly increase your odds of success. If your goal is to run or meditate for an hour a day, for example, there will probably be many days when you don't run or meditate at all. However, if you make walking around the block, or one minute of mindful breathing your goal, you can certainly accomplish that. As time goes by, you will feel proud that you've honoured your commitment to yourself. And crucially, you will have created a new neural pathway in your brain that turns your daily walk or mindfulness meditation into a habit.

ANGELS CAN FLY BECAUSE THEY CAN TAKE THEMSELVES LIGHTLY.

G. K. Chesterton

When you reach the end of your rope, tie a knot in it and hang on.

Anonymous

SAY HELLO TO YOUR FUTURE

Our minds respond strongly to visual stimulation. Surrounding yourself with images of your goals and ideal life can stimulate your emotions and fill you with the enthusiasm you need to take steps towards your dreams. A simple way to do this is to create a Vision Board of positive words and pictures that symbolise the experiences, feelings and possessions you want to attract into your life. Your 'board' could be a notice board, a folder, a scrapbook or an online pinboard. The important thing is that you fill it with images and words that excite and inspire you, such as photos, pictures from magazines, and motivational words and quotes. Your Vision Board is an image of the future, a representation of what you are working towards. Place it somewhere where you can see it every day (or set it as your homepage when you open an internet browser) and regularly visualise, affirm and believe in your goals. Have fun with the process and cherish your Vision Board – it can be a powerful catalyst in the creation of your dreams.

Sometimes you need
to take a departure
from what you do to
something that's slightly
different in order to
get inspiration.

Tori Amos

NEW HORIZONS

Travelling is one of the best ways to broaden your mind and move you out of your comfort zone. It exposes you to new cultures, enabling you to meet all sorts of people you would never normally encounter. Admittedly, we can't all afford to take a year out to travel the world, but we can holiday in new or unusual places, and plan more weekend getaways. Seek out new horizons and see how it energises your mind, body and spirit.

WONDERFUL WORKSPACES

Your workspace directly affects your productivity and creativity. Take a look around your office or home desk space. Does it inspire you and reflect who you are, or is it dull and boring? Start to notice where and when you are most creative. Do you need peace and quiet, or does chatter or music help you? Do you work best when there are no visual distractions, or do you need colour and pattern to inspire you? While it may be impractical to transform an office, you might be able to make small tweaks to your surroundings, such as hanging your favourite art or quote on the wall, moving your desk nearer to the window or placing a beautiful plant nearby. It can be hard to produce innovative work when your subconscious is saying, 'I can't work here.' An environment that suits your needs and personality can help you feel naturally inspired and motivated.

AERODYNAMICALLY, THE BUMBLEBEE SHOULDN'T BE ABLE TO FLY, BUT THE BUMBLEBEE DOESN'T KNOW SO IT GOES FLYING ANYWAY.

Mary Kay Ash

Art happens all the time, everywhere. All we have to do is to keep our minds open.

Jacek Tylicki

TAP INTO YOUR SUBCONSCIOUS

Trying to force yourself to be constantly productive and creative can be harmful to your creativity. Studies show our most creative thoughts occur when we alternate between periods of intense, focused work and rest and relaxation. This is because when our minds are calm and uncluttered, we are able to tap into our subconscious mind, which is believed to be vastly more powerful than our conscious mind. Take advantage of this by building periods of rest into your day. After you've spent some time working on a problem, take a break from what you're doing and go for a walk, meditate or stand up and stretch. Avoid watching TV or doing any activity that saturates your mind with information during this break, and instead engage in a non-stressful, physical task such as gardening, cooking or washing the dishes, as your subconscious mind works best when your conscious mind is pleasantly occupied.

The main thing is to be
moved, to love, to hope,
to tremble, to live.

Auguste Rodin

IF YOU CAN FIND
A PATH WITH
NO OBSTACLES,
IT PROBABLY
DOESN'T LEAD
ANYWHERE.

Frank A. Clark

Throw caution to the
wind and just do it.

Carrie Underwood

Better than a thousand
hollow words,
is one word that
brings **peace**.

Buddha

CONNECTING
THE DOTS

Steve Jobs talked about 'connecting the dots' in his famous Stanford commencement speech – the road ahead may seem unclear, but you can't connect the dots of your life looking forward; you can only connect them when you're looking back. In his speech he recalled how he dropped out of college and took a class in calligraphy, thinking it would have no practical application in his life whatsoever. Ten years later, he used the ideas he learned in his calligraphy class to help design the first Macintosh computer, complete with beautiful typefaces. If he had never dropped out of college he would never have taken the calligraphy class and personal computers might be vastly different today. It can be helpful to remind yourself of this story when you're struggling to reach a goal. Have faith in yourself and follow your heart, curiosity and intuition. Trust that the dots in your life will somehow connect and you will ultimately reach your dreams.

REMAIN CALM, SERENE, ALWAYS IN COMMAND OF YOURSELF. YOU WILL THEN FIND OUT HOW EASY IT IS TO GET ALONG.

Paramahansa Yogananda

EXERCISE YOUR BRAIN

Studies show that exercise stimulates the growth of new neurons in the brain. It can also boost your creativity and help you come up with new solutions to problems. Try to engage in regular physical activity such as walking, running, cycling, swimming or yoga. Aim to do something most days of the week, even if it's simply going for a brisk walk in your lunch hour. Getting in motion will boost your productivity and encourage new thought patterns and ideas.

Tension is who you
think you should
be. **Relaxation**
is who you are.

Chinese proverb

The key to everything
is patience. You get the
chicken by hatching the
egg, not by smashing it.

Arnold H. Glasow

WHAT IF?

If you're feeling stuck, a simple way to open yourself up to possibilities is to ask the question 'What if?' The words we use can influence how our brains work, so using positive statements and open questions, such as 'I can solve this', 'There's always a way' and 'What if?' can encourage lateral thinking and exploration. In contrast, negative or close-ended statements, such as 'I don't know' or 'I can't' can restrict your thinking and creativity, making it more likely that you'll remain stuck. The next time you need to come up with a solution to a problem, try using an open-ended statement such as 'What if there was a better solution to this?' Repeating this to yourself, like a creative mantra, will help your subconscious come up with answers. Try not to force a solution to appear. Relax and let inspirations and solutions emerge naturally and spontaneously.

INDULGE IN A CLASSIC

'Classic' books are called that for a reason; they have stood the test of time and are loved by readers around the world. Examples include *Pride and Prejudice* by Jane Austen, *To Kill a Mockingbird* by Harper Lee, and *On the Road* by Jack Kerouac. Google 'classic books' and pick one that takes your fancy to read this week. You'll definitely gain something from the experience; whether it's pure pleasure or insight and knowledge, the classics can enrich you in ways you didn't expect.

EVERY ARTIST WAS FIRST AN AMATEUR.

Ralph Waldo Emerson

Dream lofty dreams,
and as you dream, so
you shall become.

James Allen

He is a **wise** man who does not grieve for the things which he has not, but **rejoices** for those which he has.

Epictetus

A DAY OF RANDOMNESS

Do you sometimes find it difficult to make up your mind about trivial things, such as which restaurant to go to or which film to see at the cinema? The next time you're faced with a small choice, instead of agonising for hours, flip a coin or roll a dice and go with the answer you're given. This will free up your thinking and lead to some unexpected outcomes. Perhaps you turn left instead of right when riding your bike in a city and discover an exciting new cafe or shop, or you read a science fiction book you wouldn't normally read and realise you love the genre. Randomness can also be a useful time-saving tool. For example, if you close your eyes in a restaurant and pick an item from a menu with your finger, you can quickly get back to chatting with your friends. Dedicate a day or a weekend to making random choices. It will get you in the habit of making decisions more quickly and who knows, it may lead to one or two adventures.

YOU CAN'T USE UP CREATIVITY. THE MORE YOU USE, THE MORE YOU HAVE.

Maya Angelou

SLEEP UNDER THE STARS

Camping is a great way to reconnect with nature and leave your worries behind. Turn the TV off, leave your tablet at home (but take a mobile phone in case of emergency) and head out into the countryside or to a campsite. Take some food and a camping stove, or make your own campfire and cook dinner over an open flame. For a real sense of adventure, try sleeping under the stars in your sleeping bag, with a bivvy bag if it's cold. Camping is a cheap and easy way to open your mind to new horizons and a sense of calm.

No star is ever lost
we once have seen,
We always may be what
we might have been.

Adelaide Anne Procter

A journey of a
thousand miles begins
with a single step.

Lao Tzu

IT'S NEVER TOO LATE

Ask your parents to tell you what you were like as a child. What did you most enjoy doing? Often the things that mattered to us back then are signposts of buried dreams or activities that can fill our days with more joy. Did you used to sing at the top of your lungs, love climbing trees, or spend hours illustrating and writing stories? Can you remember your childhood dreams? Did you long to own a puppy, become a ballet dancer, or explore the Amazon rainforest? See if you can identify one or two things you used to love to do, or longed to do, and then aim to experience them now in some small way. Perhaps you could offer to walk your neighbour's dog, sign up for a dance class, or book an adventure holiday for your next trip? Whatever your secret ambition, it's never too late to reconnect with an old dream.

ONLINE INSPIRATION

There's a huge community of creative people on the internet all eager to discuss ideas and offer motivation and support. Blogs, forums and websites such as Pinterest, Twitter and Flickr allow you to follow and discuss the work of artists and innovators. Whether the medium is paint, photography, art or architecture, other people's artistic endeavours can jump-start your own curiosity and creativity. You never know, you may also meet a potential collaborator or partner for your next creative venture.

I HAVE FOUND THAT IF YOU LOVE LIFE, LIFE WILL LOVE YOU BACK.

Arthur Rubinstein

People often say that motivation doesn't last. Well, neither does bathing – that's why we recommend it daily.

Zig Ziglar

Release opinions,
free yourself from views.
Be **open** to mystery.

Jack Kornfield

THE WONDER
OF NATURE

We live on a beautiful planet, full of astounding plants and animals and yet most of us see a tiny fraction of the wonders around us. Research has shown that being in nature can help aid concentration and productivity, relieve stress and depression and give us an all-round sense of well-being, and there are lots of ways to welcome nature into your life. Fill your home with flowers, tend an allotment, and go for bracing walks in the countryside. Be like a kid again – jump in puddles, kick up leaves and forage for unusual feathers, leaves and stones. Experience the beauty of the world's oceans, forests and jungles by watching nature documentaries (even 'faking it' can give you the same benefits as the real thing). Don't forget to appreciate the plants, animals and scenery of your neighbourhood too. There is beauty all around us if we pause long enough to look. Take every opportunity to connect with nature and let it calm, strengthen and inspire you.

YOU ARE NEVER
TOO OLD TO SET
ANOTHER GOAL
OR TO DREAM A
NEW DREAM.

C. S. Lewis

FAMILY ROOTS

Uncovering your ancestors' stories can be a fascinating process which can help you understand who you are and how you fit into the bigger world around you. Do you know what your ancestors were like and what experiences they lived through? Perhaps you're related to someone famous, or someone who lived through an historic event. Look up your family tree and see what you can discover. There are several online resources that can help you with this.

Look at everything
as though you were
seeing it for the
first or last time.

Betty Smith

Life begins at the end
of your comfort zone.

Neale Donald Walsch

DREAM BIG

Achieving our goals and dreams requires energy and enthusiasm. Often the only difference between those who succeed and those who fail is that the successful carry on when the unsuccessful throw up their hands in despair and give up. A great way to keep your motivation flowing is to visualise your success in great detail. Close your eyes and imagine how your dream outcome will look, feel, smell, taste and sound. Utilise all your senses to make the experience as vivid and real as possible. Imagine where you are when you are successful.

What do your surroundings look like? Who are you with? What are you wearing? How do you feel? Form as clear a mental picture as possible and repeat this process for at least a few minutes every day. Repetition is crucial. Motivation isn't something that stays with us forever; it needs to be constantly refreshed. Daily visualisation is a powerful technique that can keep your motivation levels high over a long period of time.

A HAPPY LIFE CONSISTS NOT IN THE ABSENCE, BUT IN THE MASTERY OF HARDSHIPS.

Helen Keller

When life looks like
it's falling apart, it may
just be falling in place.

Beverley Solomon

TAKE YOURSELF ON A DATE

Taking yourself out on a 'date' can be a refreshing and liberating experience. You could sit in a cafe with a cappuccino, take a blanket and a book to the park, or enjoy a film at the cinema. Quality time alone is good for the soul and self-confidence. It can nurture your playfulness and fire up your imagination, as you revel in your own company.

If you ask me what I
came into this life to
do, I will tell you: I
came to live out loud.

Émile Zola

LOOK AT
ART SLOWLY

Visiting an art gallery or museum is a perfect antidote to a stressful week. View it as a welcome chance to slow down and calm your mind. Instead of rushing through the exhibits, pause and look carefully at each painting or sculpture. Let something grab you, even if you don't know why, and spend some time with that piece. Don't worry about understanding the meaning of the work of art; pay attention to how it makes you feel. Being fully in the moment with a work of art can improve your well-being and enhance your appreciation of the work itself – colour, beauty and pattern can speak to us and open up neural pathways in the brain that can affect us deeply. Try to visit a gallery or museum during quiet times, such as early in the morning and take time to notice and recognise your reactions.

LIFE SHRINKS
OR EXPANDS
ACCORDING TO
ONE'S COURAGE.

Anaïs Nin

BE PREPARED

You never know when inspiration will strike. Carry a notebook with you at all times so you can jot down your thoughts and ideas. You can use your notebook to record funny conversations you overhear and inspiring quotes you come across, or even sketch the cafe or bar that you're in. Leaf through your notebook whenever you're stuck for creative ideas.

The man who removes
a mountain begins
by carrying away
small stones.

Confucius

I can't change the
direction of the wind,
but I can adjust my
sails to always reach
my destination.

Jimmy Dean

A NOTE FROM THE HEART

In this age of email and text, handwritten notes are a long-lost art form, yet we all appreciate a personally written letter or card. They bring a warmth and pleasure to our world that digital communication can't replicate. Think of someone you haven't been in touch with for a while, or someone you would like to thank, and write them a handwritten note. Take some time to consider what sort of card, paper or pen would be most fitting. Whether you use a fountain pen on luxury paper, or colourful ink in a quirky card, putting pen to paper will show someone how much you care in a way that sending an email or a text never could. You'll benefit greatly too – expressing love and gratitude can help you experience better health and life satisfaction.

WATCH YOUR WORDS

We frequently use words that undermine or sabotage us. Watch how often you use words such as 'should', 'can't', 'impossible' and 'hate'. Try to omit these words from your vocabulary and use more encouraging words as you go about your day, such as 'choose', 'yes' and 'love'. Words have power. They shape our thoughts and influence our actions. Focus on positive words that fill you with hope and confidence and watch your self-belief start to soar.

FOR MYSELF I AM AN OPTIMIST – IT DOES NOT SEEM TO BE MUCH USE BEING ANYTHING ELSE.

Winston Churchill

Never underestimate
the power of passion.

Eve Sawyer

Change your
thoughts and you
change the world.

Norman Vincent Peale

ON THE MOVE

Children don't worry about 'exercise' or 'fitness' but they are constantly moving. They run, climb, squat, crawl, jump and cartwheel. As adults, we've forgotten these natural movement patterns and the increased strength, flexibility and functionality they bring. Not only do they benefit our health, they keep us feeling young, playful and confident. Start moving as much as possible throughout the day – walk in your lunch break, take the stairs rather than the lift when you're out shopping, and stretch or change position regularly when you're working at the computer. Try some fun movements – crawl or roll on the floor, balance on a safe kerb or beam, climb a rope or tree or go outside with your kids or some friends and play tag. Get creative and move more in whatever environment you find yourself in, whether that's your office, a park, your house or the gym.

IF YOU LEARN FROM DEFEAT, YOU HAVEN'T REALLY LOST.

Zig Ziglar

FACE FORWARD

You can't start the next chapter of your life if you keep re-reading the last one. Whatever has happened in the past, leave it behind you and move on. Don't allow past pains and regrets to affect the present moment and hold you back. Each day is a chance to start afresh and put your best foot forward, so focus on where you're going.

Knowledge
is limited.
Imagination
encircles the world.

Albert Einstein

As long as the mind can
envision the fact that
you can do something,
you can do it.

Arnold Schwarzenegger

THE POWER
OF SONG

Singing is good for your body and
soul. Whether you sing in the shower
or warble your way through karaoke,
singing floods our bodies with feel-
good endorphins and can boost our
confidence and self-esteem. There are
serious health benefits too. Singing
has been shown to boost our immune
system, increase our lung capacity and
increase our life expectancy. Singing
with others seems to have extra
benefits. Researchers have discovered
that choristers' heartbeats synchronise
when they sing together, resulting in

a calming effect that is as beneficial to their health as yoga. If singing in a group appeals, consider joining a choir, attending your local church, or joining a Rock Choir where you'll belt out Motown, gospel and pop classics. Whether you sing in a group or in the privacy of your home or car, singing will never fail to uplift you.

OUR LIFE IS WHAT OUR THOUGHTS MAKE IT.

Marcus Aurelius

It's the **simple things** in life that are the most **extraordinary**; only wise men are able to understand them.

Paulo Coelho

CHILDLIKE JOY

Children are experts at having fun. They have the ability to see silliness and humour in everyday things such as a trip to the shops or a walk in the woods. To learn from children, watch how freely they play. Observe how they laugh out loud and throw themselves into creative projects, such as building a sandcastle or colouring in, with great enthusiasm. Make a point of carrying their exuberant spirit with you throughout the day. Start doing things for pure enjoyment. Take time to laugh, play, dance and sing. By adopting the carefree nature of your own children, your nieces and nephews, or even the kids you see playing in the park, you can bring more joy to your life and greet each day with a smile.

BE A TOURIST IN YOUR OWN TOWN

It's easy to take your home town for granted. Are your eyes open to all the possibilities right on your doorstep? Take some time to explore your own town or city as if you were a newcomer to the area. Visit all the popular tourist sites and attractions. Check out museums, parks, cafes and art galleries you've never been to before. Curious as to where that road or path leads? Explore! Start to see your home town with fresh eyes – and don't forget your camera!

Happiness consists not in having much, but in being content with little.

Marguerite Gardiner

WRITE A HAIKU

In essence, a haiku is a short poem of three lines. It's a great way to jump in to creative writing as there are no grammatical rules and it's a far less daunting prospect than writing a short story or novel. You can write a haiku in seconds. It doesn't have to rhyme and you can write about anything – the weather, your cup of tea, or the view you see from your window. Pick your topic and let the words come to you. In order to release your inner poet, avoid over-thinking and over-planning. The aim is to use just a few words to capture a moment and create a picture in the reader's mind. Here's an example of a traditional Japanese haiku to get you started:

> old pond
> a frog leaps in
> water's sound

ONLY WHEN HE NO LONGER KNOWS WHAT HE IS DOING DOES THE PAINTER DO GOOD THINGS.

Edgar Degas

We can do anything we
want to do if we stick
to it long enough.

Helen Keller

MAKE A DIFFERENCE

Is there a cause or charity that is particularly important to you? Consider supporting an organisation that is making a positive difference in this area. There are numerous ways you can help causes you care about. You can donate financially or donate your time by volunteering. Joining an organisation or subscribing to their newsletter will ensure you receive regular updates on their work and ways you can get involved. Even helping out with the smallest tasks can make a real difference to the lives of people, animals and communities in need of help. Contact volunteer centres for opportunities and advice, as well as websites such as www.do-it.org. You can also approach community organisations directly – community theatres, museums, libraries, animal shelters, youth organisations and conservation groups are likely to welcome an extra pair of hands. Voluntary work is a great way to learn new skills, meet new people, and find a new sense of meaning and purpose in your life.

It is always the **simple** that produces the **marvellous**.

Amelia Barr

WHO ARE YOUR HEROES?

The world is filled with inspiring people who have overcome incredible odds to survive and thrive. Whatever your situation – whether you struggle with relationships, money or health – there will be someone out there who has experienced the same issue and can offer you hope, encouragement and wisdom. Seek out their stories, read their autobiographies, or watch documentaries and interviews and let their words uplift and inspire you.

YOU CAN BREAK THAT BIG PLAN INTO SMALL STEPS AND TAKE THE FIRST STEP RIGHT AWAY.

Indira Gandhi

Regret for wasted time
is more wasted time.

Mason Cooley

BEYOND
THE BRUSH

To stimulate your creativity, put down your pens and pencils and use unusual materials to create a work of art. There are all sorts of objects around the house and in nature that can be used to create interesting marks. You could dip a twig or feather into ink, or press a piece of bubble wrap into wet paint and see what marks they create, for example. Or use petals and sweet wrappers to make a colourful collage. Alternately, go back to being a kid again and just use your hands. Creating art using unfamiliar materials can help you break out of your comfort zone and move past the rules and routines that may have limited you in the past. It can encourage you to try new things and reconnect with your originality and playfulness, which can have a positive impact on all areas of your life.

Do not worry about
your originality. You
could not get rid of it
even if you wanted to.

Robert Henri

GO CONFIDENTLY IN THE DIRECTION OF YOUR DREAMS. LIVE THE LIFE YOU HAVE IMAGINED.

Henry David Thoreau

PEOPLE POWER

It's said that we are the average of the five people we spend the most time with. Take an honest look at your business and social life. Do you spend time with negative people who drain you and sap your spirit? If possible, limit your contact with these people and seek the company of happy, optimistic and successful people who will inspire you to achieve your full potential.

Life is like photography;
we develop from
the negatives.

Anonymous

BUDDY UP

Do you know a friend or colleague who wants to set a self-improvement goal or accomplish a dream? If so, consider joining them in a buddy system. Being accountable to a 'buddy' is one of the best ways to make sure you don't get distracted from your goals. By meeting regularly – weekly or monthly – you can check each other's progress, offer words of encouragement and, of course, celebrate your achievements. The system works particularly well for shared fitness goals. Going out for an early morning run may be the last thing you feel like doing when it's cold outside, but if you know your friend is waiting to meet you for a training session, you'll be forced to get out of bed. Whether you have a yoga buddy, a writing buddy or a business buddy, they need to be reliable, supportive and committed, so choose your buddy carefully. Teaming up with the right partner can dramatically increase your chances of success.

The muse visits
during the act of
creation, not before.

Roger Ebert

YOUR MIND WILL ANSWER MOST QUESTIONS IF YOU LEARN TO RELAX AND WAIT FOR THE ANSWER.

William S. Burroughs

MIND-WANDERING

You may think daydreaming is a waste of time but in fact it's a crucial part of the creative process. Your brain is not wired to be focused in a straight line all the time. Allowing your mind to wander at will can boost creativity and imagination, and even inspire great works of art and science. Woody Allen and J. K. Rowling both credit daydreaming with their best ideas. Arthur Fry came up for the idea for Post-It notes when he was daydreaming in church and Albert Einstein came up with his theory of relativity while imagining himself riding a sunbeam to the edge of the universe. Take regular breaks throughout the day and grab moments of 'down time' whenever you can – on a train journey or while waiting in a queue, for example. From now on, don't feel guilty if your thoughts start to wander; it could be the catalyst for your next big idea.

Obstacles are those
frightful things you see
when you take your
eyes off your goal.

Henry Ford

LET NATURE SOOTHE YOU

Sometimes all we need to get back on track is to spend time outdoors. When we're at one with nature, our minds can relax and our senses are reinvigorated. Take a walk in the woods, sit by a river, or lie down in the grass and feel the earth support you. Switch off your phone and take in the sights, sounds and scents of nature. Studies show the more time you spend outdoors, the greater your level of happiness and creativity.

NO COMPLAINTS

A simple way to transform your life is to stop complaining. Give it a go. Commit to one day of zero gossiping, criticising and complaining. You'll soon realise what a habit this is. We complain about the weather, the traffic, our jobs and other people. The problem is, the more we complain, the unhappier we become. This is because our brains notice more of whatever we focus on. So if you spend your days whinging and moaning, you'll always find plenty of things to complain about. Start to notice whenever you feel the temptation to make a negative comment. Some people swear by wearing a rubber band around their wrist and snapping it or switching it to the other wrist whenever they realise their thoughts have turned negative. This works as a pattern breaker – it gets your attention and brings you back to the present moment. Another trick is to simply ask yourself when you open your mouth: 'Would I rather complain or be happy?' Commit to one complaint-free day and see how much better you feel.

If you think you are
too small to make a
difference, try sleeping
with a mosquito.

Dalai Lama

THE IMPORTANT THING... IS NOT HOW MANY YEARS IN YOUR LIFE, BUT HOW MUCH LIFE IN YOUR YEARS!

Edward Stieglitz

A QUOTE A DAY

Do you have a favourite quote or saying that has got you through a hard time or inspired you to achieve a dream? Place your favourite motivational words where you can see them every day – perhaps print them out and stick them to your bathroom mirror or computer screen, or carry them with you in your bag or wallet. Surround yourself with positive thoughts, advice and ideas from the world's greatest thinkers, both past and present. Browse inspirational quotes on websites such as www.tinybuddha.com and consider buying a small book of quotes to keep by your bedside. You might even find a new favourite within the pages of this book. Dip into these sources of wisdom on a regular basis and highlight your favourite feel-good words. The right quote can shift your mindset and turn your whole day around in a second.

ASK SOMEONE HAPPY

The happiness and enthusiasm of others can be infectious. Spend time with people who possess these qualities. Ask them to tell you about the things they love most in life and watch their faces light up as they share their passions. You could even ask them what they consider to be the most important lesson they've ever learned. By listening to their words of joy and wisdom, you'll learn valuable information that you can apply to your own life.

I am seeking. I am
striving. I am in it
with all my heart.

Vincent Van Gogh

I don't measure a
man's success by how
high he climbs but
how high he bounces
when he hits bottom.

George S. Patton

ONLY THOSE
WHO WILL
RISK GOING
TOO FAR CAN
POSSIBLY FIND
OUT HOW FAR
ONE CAN GO.

T. S. Eliot

CELEBRATE HOW FAR YOU'VE COME

When life feels like an uphill struggle, focus on how far you've come, as opposed to the distance still to go. If you're running a new business, for example, instead of seeing your imperfect website and all the ideas and strategies you've yet to implement, acknowledge all the progress you have made to get to this point. Give yourself credit for your hard work and perseverance. You may not be exactly where you'd like but you've come a long way. Try writing a list of your accomplishments over the last year or two. Include progress in your self-knowledge, relationships, spirituality, health and career. Then look at your list and reflect on just how much you've achieved. Focusing exclusively on all the things you have left to do can rob you of joy and pride in your accomplishments, so from now on, celebrate how far you have come and marvel at how much your life has changed.

the little book of
HAPPINESS

lucy lane

THE LITTLE BOOK OF HAPPINESS

Lucy Lane

£5.99
Hardback
ISBN: 978-1-84953-790-2

Sometimes the hurly-burly of daily life leads our happiness levels to sink a little. But don't worry! This joyful little book is packed with inspiring quotations and simple, easy-to-follow tips that will help you unwind, relax and greet life with a smile.

the little book of
RESILIENCE

lucy lane

ISBN: 978-1-84953-830-5

the little book of
RELAXATION

lucy lane

ISBN: 978-1-84953-787-2

the little book of
POSITIVITY

lucy lane

ISBN: 978-1-84953-788-9

the little book of
MEDITATIONS

gilly pickup

ISBN: 978-1-84953-864-0

the little book of
AFFIRMATIONS

gilly pickup

ISBN: 978-1-84953-863-3

the little book of
INSPIRATION

lucy lane

ISBN: 978-1-84953-843-5

the little book of
COMFORT

lucy lane

ISBN: 978-1-84953-793-3

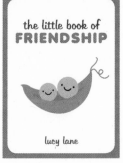

the little book of
FRIENDSHIP

lucy lane

ISBN: 978-1-84953-862-6

If you're interested in finding out
more about our books, find us on
Facebook at **Summersdale Publishers**
and follow us on Twitter
at **@Summersdale**.

www.summersdale.com